FLOURISHING FROM MENTAL ILLNESS

Memoirs of a Woman Overcoming the
Symptoms & Stigma
of her Inherited Mood Disorders

By Yolande deGastyne-Fawcett
© 2008

Cover photo by: David Coe

Inquiries may be sent to: theyoshow@bellsouth.net

To purchase copies of this book please go to:
www.TheYoShow.com or www.Lulu.com

ISBN 978-0-6151-8605-4

TABLE OF CONTENTS

ACKNOWLEDGEMENTS

First and foremost I must give thanks and praise to
my Lord and Savior Jesus Christ. It is only through
Him that I have come out of the darkness and into
the light of my life.
Secondly I want to thank my mother Raylyn Terrell,
for her skillful editing on this project.
Her abundance of time, knowledge and support
has made this book a reality.
Finally, I can't express my gratitude enough of
my husband David and children Zachary and Sierra.
Their patience, love and understanding throughout this
writing has been remarkable. I love you all!

FOREWORD

by Michele DeSouza

My Friend "Yo"

Having "Yo" in my life has been a tremendous blessing. What a fantastic individual! We met in our 20's and had fun times while we were single. I witnessed a very pretty girl who exuded such confidence and energy that I could never be down or sad when I was with her.

She could approach any potential dance partner. She could become fast friends with any gal we met. She could take on any dare and keep us cheerful and smiling all the time. I realize now, after she has patiently educated me about her illness that some of these memories of great enthusiasm may have overlapped manic episodes, but I'm not 100% sure – because the real "Yo" has an enthusiastic personality, no matter what!

Incredibly, "Yo" has rarely exposed me to the low side of her depressive episodes. To my knowledge, she never blamed anyone around her and was enduring when I might have lacked understanding.

I always admired the way she just kept going. As we got older, married and were caught up in adult responsibilities, I knew the grind of life could be very difficult for her – yet she always checked back in when her condition was stabilized.

"Yo" has given me a great example of what it means to hang-in and carry on through her hard, painful times. She was very sensitive to those around her who could not understand what was happening when she hit a rough patch.

I am thankful that I could enjoy the up times with her, but I was not aware that immensely low times might follow. Her faith and path of self-discovery have certainly opened my eyes!

INTRODUCTION

This true story is more than a declaration of a difficult life. It is a record of major events and experiences and how I have battled to overcome the incredible obstacles in my life's path. It is also amazing to realize how I survived the rigors of a troubled childhood and continue to fight the lifelong struggle of mental illness.

My audiences share in the sadness, and then become fascinated as the storyline moves through its triumphal celebration of *strength, faith and courage.* They also find *__hope__* for themselves and their loved ones, and are greatly blessed by this story of God's mercy and grace.

In my early teens I experienced bouts of pure misery, which could very quickly turn into episodes of extreme jubilation. In these early years though, I only understood the "down" side of these episodes, as depression. The "up" side was a lot more fun, but I didn't see it as a problem. After all, what could be wrong with being extremely exuberant?

At twenty-one years of age, my doctor delivered devastating news and diagnosed me as suffering from bipolar disorder, more commonly known as manic-depressive illness.

I was born fifth of seven children, each of my siblings has fought the affliction to varying degrees. This was an inheritance from our father who was diagnosed as manic-depressive in the early 1970's. The source of the mental, physical and emotional hardship I endure daily stems from a genetic "imbalance" of serotonin and other natural chemicals found in the brain.

This debilitating disorder initially surfaced when I was a freshman in high school. It quickly took control of my entire life. I was often miserably depressed and suffered through great bouts of hopelessness. Typical teen-ager and parental problems were exacerbated, and I felt no hope for a positive future, so after my fifteenth birthday, I decided to leave home and strike out on my own.

Over the years I experienced chaos that seemed to be cyclical in nature. Every three months, depressive and manic episodes would rear their ugly heads and throw me into the depths of unimaginable struggle.

In 2002, I was thirty-eight years old. My life felt very out of control and I made the scary decision to admit myself to a mental health facility. This happened twice that same year. I was frightened initially with "fear of the unknown" and the "different person" I might become once I emerged. The first stay was for the minimum of five days - so that the doctors could observe and evaluate my condition. The second visit was ten days long. This was especially difficult as it was during Easter break and I was not able to be with my two young children. Several psychiatrists and physicians closely monitored my condition.

Achieving stabilization and medication experimentation were the goals of both visits. Severe fatigue, short-term memory loss, acute insomnia, uncontrollable trembling and a weight gain of 30 pounds were the most prominent side effects of the new drugs I was prescribed. These experts also added several more labels to my mental state - Attention Deficit Disorder (ADD), Obsessive Compulsive Disorder (OCD), Self-Injury Disorder and Social Anxiety Disorder. Not being able to complete simple tasks, obsessive skin picking and shying away from social settings has made my life unbearable at times.

In the hospital I learned that educating myself on these illnesses was paramount to my recovery, and I have received incredible empowerment from the following books; The Bipolar Disorder Survivor Guide by David J. Miklowitz, PhD, You Mean I'm Not Lazy, Stupid Or Crazy?! by Kate Kelly and Peggy Ramundo and The OCD Workbook by Bruce M. Hyman, PhD and Cherry Pedrick, R.N.

Since 2005 I have been functioning at a tolerable level and daily vacillate from barely surviving to simply coping - and every once in awhile - overjoyed with tons of energy and focus. I have accepted the fact that I will need to be medicated for the remainder of my life. Prozac, Depakote, Zyprexa, Concerta and Clonazepam are the collection of medications that seem to work best for my chemical makeup.

The vision I hold for my future though, is positive. I want to be a flourishing wife, mother, writer and business owner. I must constantly gauge life events, so as not to get overwhelmed. If a high level of stress is triggered, it may result in me becoming bedridden for days.

Finally, I have found that public speaking opportunities and through writing articles, I am able to sow seeds of hope and understanding to those whose lives have been wounded by mental illness. Sharing my knowledge with others enables me to reap emotional, mental and physical strength, which in turn lightens my otherwise very heavy load.

CHAPTER ONE

Get To Know "Yo"

"Yo" at age 1

I was born on December 13, 1965 in Alexandria, Virginia and was named Yolande deGastyne. When only a few days old, I was held by my grandmother, sitting in the control room of a television station as my mother and older siblings pre-taped a Hanukah/Christmas program. At the tender age of two, I recorded the children's gospel classic, "Jesus Loves Me" and performed it live on the grounds of the Washington Monument at age four.

I was literally "born" to entertain audiences. My french father, Dr. Serge Benoist deGastyne earned a Ph.D. in music and wrote over 80 significant musical works, including six symphonies. He was also a staff composer and arranger for the United States Air Force Headquarters Band in Washington D.C. My mother, Raylyn Terrell was and still is a professional singer/songwriter, teacher and recording artist. With this inherited gene pool, I didn't have much of a choice as to where my heart would lie. My vocal talent was realized by my middle school chorus teacher and in high school; I even won a state wide singing competition.

My father left us when I was two, so I grew up in a broken home. Not coping well with the potential of having a new father every few years, I slowly created for myself a world of isolation and great sadness. I unfortunately carried this darkness into my teens and adulthood. I allowed myself to hit rock bottom when troubled and aggravated. Attitude changes, eating habits and sleeping habits were all disturbed. I felt as if I didn't belong anywhere, or to anyone. I eventually became extremely insecure and found shelter in the homes of my boyfriends.

With my family members turning into only acquaintances, school problems and mother hassles all mounting up, I had to find the ultimate release. I convinced myself that suicide was the answer to escapism. I thank God that I was able to get through that very rough patch of life, and survived to be a stronger person and a beacon of hope to others with whom I share my story.

Early in October of 1985, memories of the past three and one-half years raced through my head, as I sat on my living room couch starring out the window. The clear, cool day and my expressionless face, both attributed to my cold insides. My boyfriend Russ and I had broken our friendship/engagement the night before. We decided that we needed more freedom in our lives. We agreed to go back to dating - including others. We each had a ring to remove and we placed them on a wobbly nail on my bedroom wall, until we were ready to wear them again. It was the right thing to do, but the feeling of emptiness I felt was unbearable. I ached inside as though someone had suddenly ended my life and left me no options to take, neither heaven nor hell. Scared and confused I starred at nothing and let my mind ramble.

Unexpectedly one evening, my apartment door flew opened and in stormed husky Russ. He yelled obscenities and back fisted me across the face with force enough that landed me on the other side of the couch. The idea of dating other people was not working out well. With tear flooded eyes I swore to his eyes, "You'll never have a chance to do that again." Both of our emotions were completely out of control, but I was astonished that he had resorted to violence, as it was so unlike him. This major event at nineteen years of age I soon found was a stopping as well as starting point in my life. It was time to act my age instead of my previous adult role, and take advantage of my newly found freedom.

In high school I played varsity tennis, basketball and softball. The experience I received from the tennis team paved the way to winning a scholarship to George Mason University in Fairfax, Virginia. It was at this time that my self-esteem grew stronger and I started to reach for the stars. My positive attitude and self motivated approach to life had carried me far.

After earning a Bachelor of Science degree from <u>GMU</u>, I quickly put my amateur entertainment status to rest, and began performing in night clubs around the beltway area. I had been taught that having "that piece of paper," was essential to having a successful future. I never lost sight of that and still today encourage teens to stay in school and apply to colleges.

1988 Bachelor of Science Degree

It was also at this time that I took a couple quick trips to New York, Nashville, and Los Angeles to pursue a singing career.

Grand Ole Opry Parking Lot

Audition Studio in New York City

It was the 1st of September in 1991 at 9:30 A.M., when I said goodbye to my fiancé Nick, as he headed off to work. He was very supportive and encouraging of my efforts to "make it big." We had shared a five and one-half year, on again off again, dating relationship.

It had taken a month to prepare for a cross country trip to California. My biggest concerns were the bills I was leaving behind with Nick. Since I wasn't going to have a steady job for a while, I didn't want my debts to become a burden for him. He assured me though that everything would be alright.

So, equipped with a micro-cassette tape recorder in hand and my Toyota Tercel, I prepared to embark on my journey to find mega-stardom. The mileage on my car read 7,444 as I set out in pursuit of my dream, to become a famous singer. Part of this dream was to someday meet and sing a duet with Peter Cetera, Luther Vandross, Michael W. Smith or Phil Collins.

As I began to drive west on Virginia's Rt. 66, I thanked the Lord for his guidance and prayed that He would keep me safe. Unfortunately, the untimely death of one of Nick's closest friends, brought me back to Virginia prematurely. This tumultuous period in our lives also proved to be the ultimate demise of our engagement.

In 1992 I found love once again with my boyfriend Matthew. We shared a wonderful year together, until I increasingly grew depressed (for no apparent reason.) One night in particular I was emotionally unstable. I began to panic and experienced a mighty anxiety attack. This episode brought our relationship to a sudden end.

Soon after in 1993 I decided to move to Atlanta, Georgia, the fourth largest music industry center in the nation. I threw a going away party for myself and actually invited three of my ex-boyfriends, who all actually came! I prepared for another road trip and took a second stab at stardom and husband shopping.

Off to find a new life in Atlanta, Georgia.

Fawcett Family 2004

It was in Atlanta, that I started a disc jockey and karaoke service, which quickly earned me a glowing reputation as one of the city's premier entertainers. I also finally found "Mr. Right", and married my husband David Fawcett, in 1994. Together we are the proud parents of two wonderful children, Zachary and Sierra.

CHAPTER TWO
Papa

Sgt. Serge deGastyne

Gravesite at Arlington
National Cemetery

I was two years old when my father, or Papa as we called him, left my mother. She had not yet given birth to my third brother. As the years passed, I saw Papa only a few times, so I was never able to develop a relationship with him.

During my senior year in high school I was given the opportunity to connect with my estranged father, by way of an assignment in my history class. I was instructed to interview someone with knowledge of the French culture. Even though I barely knew the man, I thought: who better to research than someone who grew up in France. He accepted my invitation, although I'll admit at first, I was very uncomfortable.

He lived about a mile away from us and I went to his tiny run down house, every day for a week. We actually started to bond and I was pleasantly surprised! We worked on the project and learned about each other at the same time. He told me some shocking stories about how hard it was, not being attached to his children. I was amazed and almost frightened when he said that at times he would lie on his living room floor in front of a fire and curse himself to sleep.

He also told me that when I was very young and on one of my Thanksgiving visits to see him, he overheard me talking to my sister. I had told her that I had been invited to go to the movies with a friend, but couldn't go because I had to visit my father. Papa made the decision then and there to never interfere with his children's lives again.

I had been busy with other school activities and had not been able to come by for project work for a couple of weeks. The next time I did go remains a horrible memory. I was walking up his broken sidewalk when the screen door was thrown open. Papa stood in the doorway and yelled at the top of his lungs, "You are a spoiled little brat! You're just like your mother! Get out of my life! I never want to see you again!" He still had a very strong French accent and that made his message even more effective. Spoiled though? Like my mother? I didn't see the connections. I have come to understand now though, that this was a manic episode manifested by anger.

I was terrified, but I did not back down. "Where do you get off talking to me like that?" I yelled back. I was hurting terribly and the tears cut loose. I told him where to go and then I jumped in my car and sped off. Suicidal thoughts consumed me and I raced top speed down the George Washington Parkway. I was crying hysterically and was totally out of control. Gradually, as sanity began to return, I decided to pull the car over and pull myself together. I sat on the bank of the Potomac River and let my nerves settle.

As I increasingly learn more about my illness and its genetic links, I have become compassionate when I think about my father. In addition, I have gained knowledge of his life time achievements. I was a young adult when he died and I'm glad that I attended his funeral. Today when I speak of or think of him, I am full of admiration and pride. After all, I wouldn't have ever been born if it weren't for him and my mother. The man who was my Papa...was born and grew up in France...outwitted the Nazi's and survived the French occupation in WWII...became an accomplished pianist and composer...came to America and joined the Air Force...married my mother and gave me some amazing siblings!

CHAPTER THREE

Learning About My Illnesses

Contemplating suicide overlooking the Blue Ridge Mountains in Shenandoah, VA.

As defined by the renowned Mayo Clinic: a person with bipolar disorder swings from emotional highs to emotional lows. They will vacillate from euphoria to depression and juggle the up and down cyclical changes of recklessness to listlessness. These are the extremes associated with bipolar disorder, which can be serious and a disabling mental illness.

The condition is also known as manic-depressive illness which covers a spectrum of behaviors from grandiose manias on the one extreme, to an unbearable black hole of depression on the other. Its causes are elusive, and there is no cure. But it can be managed. Left untreated, the condition usually worsens. The flares of bipolar disorder may last for weeks or months, causing great disturbances in the lives of those affected, their friends and their families.

I have come to learn that doctors and researchers don't know exactly what causes bipolar disorder. But a variety of biologic, genetic and environmental factors seem to be involved in causing and triggering episodes of the illness. Differences in the chemical messengers between nerve cells in the brain called neurotransmitters, occur in people who have bipolar disorder. The abnormality may be in genes that regulate neurotransmitters. This is the case with me and many of my family members. According to The Mayo Clinic, a family history appears to exist in about 60 percent of cases of bipolar disorder. Researchers are attempting to identify genes that may make people susceptible to this disorder.

Factors that may contribute to or trigger episodes of bipolar disorder can include drug or alcohol abuse and stressful or psychologically traumatic events. Thankfully, I have never abused drugs or alcohol, but I have known others with this disorder who do try to self medicate. Eventually it only intensifies and worsens their condition.

When I am in the manic phase of this illness, the signs and symptoms I experience include: feelings of euphoria, extreme optimism, inflated self-esteem, rapid speech and increased physical activity. One minute I may be feeling completely fatigued. The next thing I know, I am up and mowing the lawn, catching up on the household laundry, hitting the mall, spending joyful and active moments with my children or even "championing a cause," as seen below.

DAVID SPENCER/Staff Photographer

Yolande Fawcett stands by a makeshift traffic barricade she set up in front of her house on Pine Lake Drive to make a point about potential congestion in her North River Shores neighborhood.

Public demonstration against urban sprawl

Mania can also cause poor judgment which can lead me to make unwise decisions. My most notable symptoms are racing thoughts, agitation, recklessness, a tendency to be easily distracted, an inability to concentrate, and extreme irritability. More in-depth examples of this behavior are discussed in chapter five.

When I am in the depressed phase, signs and symptoms include: persistent feelings of sadness, anxiety, guilt, hopelessness, disturbances in sleep and appetite, severe fatigue, loss of short-term memory, lack of interest in daily activities, difficulty in concentrating and in severe episodes, recurring thoughts of suicide. To "escape," I simply shut down, hide in my bed and sleep for hours or days on end until the heavy mood has lifted.

The signs and symptoms I experience with Obsessive Compulsive Disorder (OCD) are extremely intrusive to my everyday life. For example, since moving to Florida, I have become obsessed with palm trees - I **LOVE** them! If I happen to see something with a palm tree theme in a store, it is extremely difficult for me to walk away from it. Thus, my home is "overly" decorated with palm trees in as many forms as you can possibly imagine; candles, bedding, clocks, calendars, silk plants, photo albums, wall art, kitchen and bath accessories, etc.

Compulsions are the action I take as a result of the obsession. These are repetitive behaviors that I am driven to perform regularly. I have an excessive concern with order, symmetry and exactness and will often find myself arranging items in precise order; or straightening a crooked picture on a wall for example. I also deal with excessive hand washing. I don't necessarily fear germs, but I have learned that other sufferers find possible contamination overwhelming. I simply need clean hands at all times.

A more dangerous side of this illness is when my mind and body are daily bombarded with negative impulses such as picking at my skin. I excessively pluck my eye-brows and constantly pick acne on my face. Most of all, I am appalled and disgusted by the lack of control I have over scratching and picking bug bites, digging out ingrown hairs and cutting gray hair that is increasingly invading my head.

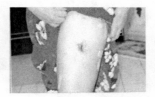

Self Injury

After performing these and other rituals, I feel some relief from anxiety, but not for long. Soon the discomfort returns and I am compelled to repeat the negative behaviors. These repetitive thoughts and behaviors are frustrating, but I can't free myself from them. I am able to control unwanted behaviors for a day or so, but my resistance weakens quickly.

As if the actions themselves weren't bad enough, it is the fact that these rituals take up a huge amount of time daily, making it virtually impossible to lead a "normal" life.

During times of high stress, I notice my symptoms becoming more severe. When I was thirty-nine, I was wrestling with some difficult family issues, while at the same time, dealing with intense pressures from work. This brought on periodic dyslexia. I would reverse numbers and letters on work contracts and other papers of importance. I even found myself reversing the elevator buttons in my office building. That was scary!

I try very hard to monitor and regulate my stress levels, so that I don't find myself in a dangerous tailspin. Becoming completely overwhelmed is a recipe for disaster. I recall some sort of emotional crash at work one day and verbally lashed out at an associate. I stormed out of the office in a bizarre manner and was gone for two hours, which left everyone in the office worrying. This behavior was completely foreign to me. I'm not going to lie to you; it was terrifying to be out of control like that.

Late that same year, I was working in sales full time. When I forgot to include vital information on several contracts; neglected to write important things in my date planner, missed an appointment with a client, and simply forgot to bring the kids' lunches to school, I realized that I couldn't handle my work load and decided to quit my job before the start of the New Year.

Short-term memory loss is one of the most frightening symptoms I acquire under extreme stress. I recall losing a $50 bill that was given to me as a gift. I also lost my keys - then - misplaced and re-found the second set! This behavior is very odd, as I consider myself to be a very organized and responsible person.

My young daughter likened me to Dori, the blue fish from the movie Finding Nemo. This character was very funny, but also had a terrible case of short-term memory loss. Forgetfulness can be humorous at times, but not when it becomes the cause of neglect.

I remember one week in particular that was extremely difficult and embarrassing. I wasn't able to recall my pharmacist's name, although I spoke with her regularly. I couldn't recall weekend activities, when asked about them on the subsequent Monday. When I would read I couldn't retain the content, I had to read things over and over again. One day I was in the Publix grocery store and ended up carrying on a long conversation with someone who seemed to know me very well, yet I had "no idea" as to who <u>she</u> was. To this day, I still can't figure that one out!

Extreme attacks of fatigue are a daily battle for me. It is arduous as it is not only a symptom of depression, but also a side effect of my medications. I shut down both physically and mentally. A simple caffeine boost doesn't even help when I'm in this state. I have found that a power nap for one hour on the floor is essential to recharge my system and to see me through the remainder of the day.

I still wrestle with skin picking. My legs look disgusting and I have a very poor self-image. Excessive concern with order, symmetry and exactness, as well as checking and re-checking everything I do, continues to stifle my daily life. In addition, getting out of bed in the morning is extremely difficult because of heavy and achy legs. Also, weight gain, feeling apathetic and dealing with short-term memory loss - continue to try my patience. This being said though, I am at a "good" place with my illnesses. I am happy, fairly functional and am looking to the future in a positive light.

CHAPTER FOUR

Get A Job

As if getting and keeping a job isn't tough enough for the average person, try adding a mental illness to the mix. Most individuals who suffer from bipolar disorder find it extremely difficult to find long-term work, and more importantly, work that they enjoy. Thankfully the symptoms of my illnesses didn't expose themselves until I was in my twenties.

As a young child I was blessed to develop a good work ethic. Growing up in Virginia, we enjoyed all four seasons, so I was able to earn money and learn several jobs in the outdoors. I mowed lawns, raked leaves, washed cars, and even had a paper route delivering the Washington Star.

When I turned fifteen years of age, I was able to get a workers-permit. My first "real" job was a line worker in the kitchen of a seafood restaurant. I remember coming home smelling like a fish and not being able to escape the odor for days. The pay wasn't that great either; I believe minimum wage at that time was around $3.00 per hour. I did however; acquire an appreciation for eating seafood and learning of its health benefits.

When I left home my sophomore year in high school, I entered a government co-op program through the school. I worked for the Directorate of Combat Developments at the Fort Belvoir Army Base. My duties were primarily typing and filing for my boss who was a Major. My favorite memory of this job is when I was selling submarine sandwiches for a school fundraiser. An enlisted man in another division ordered a sub from me, but refused to pay when I delivered it. My boss immediately called him and said, "I will personally kick your behind and report you to your commanding officer if you don't pay this young lady what you owe her." That was how I learned the power of "pulling rank." My mornings were obligated by the duties of this job and afternoons were left for attending classes and competing on the school tennis team.

In my early college years I recall trying to hold down seven jobs at the same time, and tried desperately to make it to classes on time. Christmas break was approaching my first year and I worked in the local mall for three different companies. I demonstrated and sold hair accessories, sprayed cologne and perfume samples on the passersby, and strolled through JC Penney's in an elf suit singing Christmas carols. I also worked two jobs through the Salvation Army. I braved the cold, rang their famous bell and sang Christmas carols while collecting money for the needy. I also managed their public gymnasium. In addition I juggled my schedule to be able to work as a secretary/receptionist for several temp agencies, as well as performing night gigs with one of my brothers.

One of the best jobs I ever had came towards the end of my college years. It was an internship with a racquet and health club. Management there had me learn the inner workings of the club and appointed me to work in every department. It was fantastic! I learned that I had a knack for marketing, as I enjoyed that department the most. They even let me put together an entire racquetball tournament from start to finish. The best thing about it though, was that it was worth 12 college credits which put me on the Dean's list for the first time in my life.

After the internship was completed I was lucky enough to find an administrative assistant position supporting the vice president of a public relations firm. This experience was invaluable. At one point, he left the firm to start his own company and he took me with him! This job lasted several years and he even co-signed the contract for my first new car.

One day in my early twenties I popped into a slummy pawn shop on Route 1 in Alexandria, Virginia. I had very little money, so I made the tough decision to give up some very sentimental things in exchange for cash. The first item was my college class ring. It was gold and had two small diamonds in it. It wasn't really worth very much, but to me it signified the personal resolve and resilience I demonstrated during those difficult four years. I also had a couple of gold chains and some antique items that my grandmother had left me.

The gentleman behind the counter could see how upset I was and he actually tried to console me. He said, "Keep your chin up, I'm sure things will turn around." I was surprised to learn that the establishment had a loan process, and that by paying interest, I would be able to get the items back. I originally thought once you pawned something, it was gone for good. I walked out of the store with $82.00, still feeling very sad, and trying to fight back tears.

Earlier that same day I had received and attached personalized license plates for my car. The letters spelled out - TNK PSTV (Think Positive.) As I pulled out of the parking lot, I looked in my rear view mirror and saw the pawn clerk and his associate pointing to my tags and giving me a smile and a "thumbs up!"

My life's motto!

One of the things that launched my hunger to reach for the stars, was when I was singing the National Anthem for George Mason University athletic events. I had been performing it for three years, but one night in particular really stands out. Five minutes before I went out on to the court, I was told that Tom Selleck (Magnum P.I.), was in the crowd. He had come to watch his son play in an NCAA volleyball tournament. CBS cameras were there as well, and I was on cloud nine!

My boss pointed him out to me and sure enough, Tom Selleck was in the stands. I couldn't believe that a famous movie and TV star was going to hear me sing. Once I was handed the microphone, I wanted to say, "This one's for you Tom," but I kept my composure and remained professional. I put my heart into it and gave the performance of my life. I was glad that I had earlier chosen to wear a long skirt, as my knees were shaking uncontrollably.

I was determined to meet Mr. Selleck, but security kept him protected so that he could enjoy the tournament. So I came up with a plan to leave my Mary Kay Cosmetics business card in the driver's window of his limousine. I wrote on the back that I was the national anthem singer that night, and that I hoped he enjoyed his stay in Virginia.

Three months later, my roommate Nicole was bringing in the mail, that included a large envelope from Universal Studios. She started screaming excitedly as I came to see what all the commotion was about. To our amazement, it was an autographed 8x10 glossy of Tom Selleck. He even included a personal note saying that he would be happy to help me with my singing career, although his contacts were primarily in film.

We did exchange further correspondence. I told him about my interest in appearing on the Arsenio Hall Show, but he tried to encourage me to take the route of getting an agent and auditioning for Star Search. I avoided that course of action because I had heard many horror stories about bad agents who were simply money hungry. I didn't trust anyone in the entertainment industry and refused to get an agent until I absolutely had to have one.

That same year I went to the Bobby Poe Music Survey's annual celebrity cocktail party. I had attended this networking function twice before with hopes of meeting the right folks – hi-profile people who had the ability to make and break careers in the entertainment field. The party was primarily for radio and record company executives, but there were always celebrities on hand to spice up the atmosphere. I met the likes of John Cougar Mellencamp, Vanessa Williams and Lenny Kravitz.

I had recently made a promotional music video, and hoped to get it into the right hands. The representative from Motown Records watched it and just smiled politely. I did however find a DJ from Warner Bros. Records who was showing new artist videos in one of the hotel suites. I didn't get anywhere with him, until a man I had met earlier in the evening got the ball rolling for me. He handed my video to the DJ and quickly said, "I have to catch a plane in half an hour and I need to see this video before I go…you've got to see this "Yo" girl." "Put it on **next**!"

Sure enough the disc jockey put it on the giant screen and there I was, for everyone to see. A buzz of enthusiastic curiosity filled the room. As everyone stopped talking, I watched facial expressions and listened to the comments all around me. "Who is this girl, what is this?" It was a massive "high" for me; I'd never had that experience before. Then I started to get nervous as so much attention had been drawn to it. It was then that a voice shouted out, "Who is that, get that off the screen!" And that was that, but it was so worth it.

Also there were celebrities from the sports world. While in line at the buffet table, I was waiting for sliced roast beef and noticed real "Beef Cake" standing right behind me. It was none other than number 44, John Riggins from the Washington Redskins, of whom I was a huge fan! I was feeling rather obnoxious and don't exactly know why, other than feeling manic, but I decided to sock him in the shoulder. His plate full of food wobbled, but thankfully did not fall. He poised himself for a punch back until he noticed that I was just a little girl, compared to his massive frame. He then got in my face and said "Young lady, you have got some nerve!" I introduced him to my girlfriend and we were buddies for the rest of the night.

When I couldn't take another record company door shutting in my face, I found a sales job and did quite well selling cellular car phones and service plans.

In 1993 I moved to Atlanta, Georgia. My plan was to continue in sales. An offer didn't come quickly so I was forced to get creative. One morning I got up early and dressed in my best "power suit." I went to a local Krispy Kreme donut shop and bought ten dozen boxes of their famous glazed variety. The plan was to stand outside of a prominent business center and unload the donuts, while I advertised that I was looking for work. I got off to a good start, but it didn't last. After the first box was sold, I went to the curb to pick up the next one and found that a colony of ants had already infested my remaining inventory. I was devastated!

I finally did receive a job offer with another cellular phone company. I worked that job for six months until the day when I went in during the wee hours of the morning, cleared my desk out and left a note for my boss. I had met a special man who had convinced me to go away with him to forget my stress and troubles for a while. This man eventually became my husband, David.

Just after we got married, David believed in me enough to start up two home based businesses; a mobile disc jockey service and a secretarial service. My slogans were, *"For the Party of Your Life...Call the Life of Your Party"* and *"I'll Assess Your Mess & Turn Your Piles Into Files.*" I had finally found my work destiny. After fourteen years I still love what I do and business is still going strong!

CHAPTER FIVE

Bipolar Disorder – Depression & Manic Mayhem

Depression is a disorder that affects thoughts, moods, feelings, behavior and physical health. There was a time when the public at large thought it was just "all in your head" and that if you really tried, you could "pull yourself out of it." Doctors now know that depression is not a weakness and you can't treat it on your own. They also acknowledge that it is an actual medical illness with a biological and chemical foundation.

Often, stressful life events can trigger depression. Other times depression seems to occur spontaneously, with no identifiable specific cause. Whatever the cause, depression is much more than grieving or a bout of the blues.

Depression may occur only once in a person's life. However, my personal experience has been a lifetime of scarring with repeated episodes, and periods free of depression in between. My condition is chronic and requires ongoing treatment. This illness affects more than 18 million Americans of all ages and races. Medications are available that are generally safe and effective, even for the most severe depression. With proper treatment, most people with serious depression improve, often within weeks and can return to normal daily activities.

There is no single cause for depression. Psychiatrists do agree that the illness often runs in families - thus - the genetic link. Researchers have identified several genes that may be involved in bipolar disorder, and they're looking for genes linked to other types of depression. But not everyone with a family history of depression develops the disease. They have pin pointed environmental factors such as stress and physical illness, and concur that these can trigger an imbalance of the brain chemicals serotonin, norepinephrine and dopamine. Stressful life events, particularly a loss or threatened loss of a loved one or a job, can trigger depression. Scientists don't yet fully understand how imbalances in neurotransmitters cause signs and symptoms of depression. It's not certain whether changes in neurotransmitters are a cause or a result of depression.

I was a freshman in high school when I believe I had my first manic episode, although at the time I just thought I was simply being rebellious. I had just gotten over a two week stomach illness caused by nervousness, when I could not eat, sleep or concentrate in school because I was constantly in the bathroom. My mother and I were constantly butting heads, and I was aggravated to such a point, that I planned a hideous deed. It was 2:00 A.M. when I crawled out of my ground floor bedroom window into a silent world, except for the sound of chirping crickets which annoyed me.

The air was thick and my hands were completely sweaty by the time my feet hit the dewy grass. Wrapped up in my shirt were eight rolls of toilet paper and one dozen eggs. I bombarded my own house!

It was quite a masterpiece, until the first rain came and washed it all away. I felt awful though because my mother made my two younger brothers clean up all the limp, saturated pieces which had fallen to the yard. I was pleased with my performance just the same. Three months later I was having feelings of guilt and turned myself in. Mom told me that she knew I was the "TP & Egg" bandit all along. So much for the perfect crime.

My freshman year of college was quite stressful, as I was working full time to support myself, attending classes trying to make good grades and playing competitive tennis on GMU's tennis team. Restful sleep was hard to come by and I remember one night in particular that insomnia played king.

It was cold outside and I was studying for exams before the winter break. Midnight passed and I couldn't concentrate a minute longer, but couldn't fall asleep either. All of a sudden I got an idea which was accompanied by a huge burst of energy. I devised a plan to make my mark on the campus quad for the morning students and professors. The snow was coming down like rain and I decided to make a giant "YO" out of snow. I bundled up and loaded my boom-box with batteries. It wasn't until 3:00A.M. that I packed it in and tried to go back to bed.

I also recall another manic episode where I impulsively hopped a plane to California intending to "get discovered" by a record company. I had just been given my first credit card and I used it to get $6,000.00 in debt in less than two days. The ride there was wonderful, especially since my seat mate was a good looking, minor league baseball player. We talked for hours and when we landed, he invited me to stay with him in his hotel room. I was young and impressionable. His demeanor started to change once he had me alone and I got scared. When he went into the bathroom I snuck out of the hotel. I contacted a cousin who lived in California and was most thankful to have my life and dignity still intact as she came to my rescue.

Nearing the end of college, I found myself in another manic mode and displayed a terrible lack in judgment. I was on my way home from work, stuck in bumper to bumper traffic on the Washington Beltway. I played a game of tag with four girls in a convertible, who were loud and verbal about being on their spring break. They were from Syracuse University. Written on their car were statements like, ROAD TRIP and DAYTONA or BUST!

I had never been able to enjoy a spring break in college because I had to work on all the holidays to pay for school. I was feeling sorry for myself and incredibly jealous of these girls who seemed to be so carefree of all responsibility. Out of the blue one of them yelled, "Come with us!" I barely gave it a second thought and said, "OK!" They couldn't believe it, but I was pumped. I was really going to follow them to Daytona Beach, Florida - right then and there.

It was a very long drive from Virginia to Florida and I had a lot of time to mentally process how completely irresponsible this decision was. We stopped at the tourist trap South of the Border, to hit the bathroom and load up on junk food. When we rallied back to the cars, I found a man's leg sticking out from the front end of my Toyota. I yelled at him to get out and kicked him several times. He tried to play it off like he thought it was his car, and he was looking for his hide-a-key that was attached to the front wheel well. What's scary is that I did hide a spare key in that very same spot and if I had stayed in the store much longer, I might have had my car stolen and no way to get home. I can't tell you how sick in the stomach that made me feel!

We continued on and I even invited a couple of the girls to ride with me for a change of pace. They agreed and we shared a lot about each other. They thought I was absolutely wacko, but loved my care-free spirit even more. Still wearing my business suit with no packed bags or toiletries, I followed their convertible into the parking lot of their motel. Night had fallen and all of a sudden, a giant wave of reality, guilt and anxiety consumed me. As I look back I believe that this was my first experience with anxiety attacks. The realization of what I had done and how irresponsible it was, left me in tears and literally gasping for air. I said goodbye to the party girls and headed back to Virginia, alone, on the ten hour drive.

In June of 2001, my husband David woke in the middle of the night, to find me sprawled out on the living room floor. He said, "It's 2:00A.M., what are you doing?" My answer left him dumfounded.

The Andrea Yates story, (the woman who drowned her five children) was all over the news and I felt a weird connection to it. Not that I had to come to her defense because she was mentally ill, but because I **HAD** to raise money for her husband Rusty who had to plan funerals and bury his children. So I was busy making posters to wear on my front and back side. I went out into the morning rush hour traffic and actually collected about fifty dollars. When people asked how I was going to get the money to him, I simply said that CNN would find the right contact, and that they did.

When my children were five and six, I was struggling daily with extremely frustrating symptoms of depression. My husband was working regular day time hours and to pick up my slack, he also cooked dinner and attended to the children when he got home. Can you imagine unloading that much additional stress to someone's day? Since my care for them was not what it should be, the guilt was all consuming and I often cursed myself for it.

My husband is a great father and provider for our family, yet the irritability I experienced from premenstrual symptom (PMS) was "off the charts!" I couldn't stand to look at, speak to, or interact with him until the black mood had lifted. Thankfully, the children were much less affected by this symptom. There was virtually no joy in my life. The only time I felt happiness was when either of my children smiled or gave me a hug.

We often missed the school bus or arrived late, as it was so difficult for me to physically get out of bed. I was overwhelmed with the papers that came home in their backpacks. Sometimes I didn't even get the appropriate papers back to their teachers in a timely fashion.

I was constantly sleeping and was only awake about six to seven hours a day. It was extremely difficult to accomplish the most simple of tasks: getting out of bed, taking a shower, dressing myself, getting the mail, answering the phone, washing dishes, doing laundry, etc. Most days these things never got done. At night I was so fatigued, it was virtually impossible for me to even make sure that the children had brushed their teeth. Now we're paying for that with stressful and expensive trips to the dentist.

At this point in my treatment, I was taking two anti-depressants to combat depression and severe irritability. Although we thought at the time that Prozac and Wellbutrin were a good combination for my particular issues, it gradually became clear that I needed another experiment with medication.

A manic moment in "Hotlanta" on the MARTA railway system!

Many people who suffer from bipolar disorder decide to self medicate themselves with alcohol and/or drugs. A byproduct of this decision can bring on anger and acts of violent behavior, especially in men. I often thank God for keeping my family and me safe from harm, as most of my personal experiences with mania could be viewed as funny, if they weren't actually the result of my illness. The down side of mania for me is that it affects my judgment and causes me to make impulsive and unwise decisions. Take spending money for example; David has several times, needed to take away my credit card, until I was once again stable and could use it responsibly. I experience feelings of euphoria, extreme optimism and inflated self-esteem. Other signs of my manic episodes are rapid speech, racing thoughts, agitation, increased physical activity, difficulty sleeping, inability to concentrate and extreme irritability.

CHAPTER SIX

Medication Experimentation

__Note from the Author__ - (The information in this chapter and other medical information throughout the book, is simply an account of my own personal experience and is in no way a recommendation for readers. Please seek the advice of _your_ doctor before trying any medications.)

I was living in Virginia in 1986, when I was first diagnosed with bipolar disorder. I learned that it was hereditary and that I would probably struggle with it for the remainder of my life. I sought help from an M.D. who prescribed the anti-depressant Zoloft. Unfortunately, only one side of my illness received treatment. I was given medication for depression only and my manic side was initially left to fend for itself. I was a twenty-one year old college student, and was going through a difficult breakup with my boyfriend at the time. After several months, I discontinued use of this medication because it caused intense headaches.

In 1992, I abruptly moved to Atlanta, Georgia to leave behind the collection of heartaches and sadness of my life in Virginia. In retrospect, I have come to understand that the quick and impulsive decision to start a new life elsewhere - was a manic episode in and of itself. I have learned that mania can consist of grandiose thoughts and a false sense of security. I must say though that I was truly blessed to quickly find a psychologist who was very sensitive and compassionate about my mental, physical and emotional wellbeing. She strongly urged me to start a medication regimen of Prozac to treat my depression and Wellbutrin to control my mania. After several weeks, this combination did prove to stabilize and balance my system. I was obedient and took the medication daily.

I stopped taking "the Pill" in 1995, as I was now married and wanting to have children. It was also at this time I learned that premenstrual syndrome (PMS), was an <u>actual</u> phenomenon. I was on "the Pill" for over ten years and not until I had stopped taking it, did I experience abdominal cramping, heavy bleeding, moodiness and severe irritability. The next year my husband and I were blessed with our first born, Zachary. I did display a touch of post-partum depression, but it wasn't serious. My ob/gyn strongly recommended that I get back on the Wellbutrin and Prozac regimen, so I did.

Our chaotic move to Florida in 2002 placed my mental wellbeing in a state of massive upheaval and turmoil. For starters, the first psychiatrist I found in town that accepted my insurance was a nightmare. He added ADD, OCD and Social Anxiety Disorder to my diagnosis. On my first visit to his office, he prescribed a huge mix of drugs that I had never been exposed to. The result was devastating and eventually put me in a mental health hospital. For the first time in my life, I accepted and truly understood the magnitude of my illness. He prescribed Paxil to treat my depression. The major side-effect of this drug increased my appetite which caused a thirty pound weight gain in just two weeks time. It also caused insomnia. My self-esteem took a dive and I abruptly stopped taking the Paxil.

Lithium was prescribed to treat the manic stage of my bipolar disorder. On this drug I suffered diarrhea, drowsiness, lack of coordination, loss of appetite, muscle weakness, nausea, slurred speech, and severe trembling. I was too miserable to complete the ramp up dosing period and decided that this wasn't the one for me either. Lamictal was used in tandem to act as an anti-seizure medication. Instead of protection, it provided severe clumsiness, dizziness, drowsiness, dryness of mouth and slurred speech. Since I stopped taking the Lithium, thank God there was no longer a need for the Lamictal.

The primary reason for my illness is an imbalance of the natural brain chemical called "Serotonin." This imbalance prevents neurotransmitters to properly connect. Neurotransmitters are chemical messengers which enable nerve cells to communicate. Variations in neurotransmission that can control mood and emotion, very often cause depression & other undesirable conditions.

In the spring of 2003, I was re-admitted to the mental facility for ten days. Although being away from my family that long was difficult, I came out of the experience with a new combination of medications that better treated my chemical imbalance. I found a new and outstanding psychiatrist to boot!

It was then that I accepted the fact that I would need to be medicated for the remainder of my life. A blend was prescribed of Lexapro to treat the depression, Depakote to manage the mania and Adderall to treat my "newly" diagnosed disorder of Attention Deficit Disorder (ADD). Through a lot of reading and wonderful communication with my psychiatrist, we also discovered some symptoms of Obsessive Compulsive Disorder (OCD). The approach we agreed upon to combat this illness was through behavioral therapy, as opposed to adding a fourth drug to my system. I believe that I've always had a mild case of OCD, but I also believe that the majority of its symptoms are side effects of my medications.

In 2004 on a monthly basis, I tried to track the symptoms and/or side effects I was experiencing. The following are my findings.

January – Heightened sense of smell. It was also at this time that I wanted to see what would happen if I stopped taking the Depakote and quit cold turkey. This experiment was nothing short of stupid, as I went through some extremely intense withdrawal symptoms and became very, very ill. I learned the hard way that I had to slowly be weaned off of that medication. (Don't **EVER** stop or start taking medications without your doctor's orders.)

February – OCD symptoms kicked into high gear with the incessant scratching and scraping of bug bites, in grown hair and acne mostly on my legs and buttocks. This constantly left open sores which I wouldn't allow to heal. Eventually they became infected.

March – One morning I started plucking my eyebrows and ended up pulling out three quarters of each brow. I was simply not able to stop! I was also obsessed with symmetry and found myself constantly adjusting picture frames on walls. Another annoying symptom was the mammoth piles I would build from bills, receipts and other papers that would stay un-filed until I had an energized moment to properly put them away. Most disturbing though, was the intense awareness I had of the need for my children's faces to be clean. I was constantly checking and wiping their eyes, nose and ears.

April – My period came later than usual this month. As soon as it arrived though, I noticed an **immediate** hormonal shift. I had a much needed bowel movement, but more importantly, I was talkative and cheerful with David. There wasn't the slightest bit of "irritability" to be found! This observable fact has happened repeatedly for as long as I've been tracking my symptoms. I frequently prayed, "If only there was a way to simulate my body's chemistry on period day - I would no longer suffer from my illnesses." It is on this day every month; I like and can even love myself. I feel as if I am the wonderful person God made me to be. I am the best wife to David on this day, I am the best mother to Zachary and Sierra on this day, I am the best communicator to my friends on this day and I run my business the most effectively on this day. Not to mention, I feel closer to my Creator on this day and am able to pray to Him and thank Him genuinely for all of the blessings in my life! Now that is significant - I truly wish that there was a way to bottle this.

Obviously there is something related hormonally to my chemical makeup. During my menstrual cycle I am rewarded with restful sleep and wake up in the morning with "normal" energy, enough to take a shower. This is not something I am able to do most days of the month. I also find that I am not overcome with the intense urge to cut my gray hairs when I see them in the mirror. Additionally, I am more interested in bandaging and healing my leg wounds, than scratching and scraping them open. I thank God for this too, for my tool which was once simply a fingernail, has now become a sharp cuticle cutter. I actually found myself "speeding" a little bit because of the mixture of "a good chemical balance," the Adderall, and a cup of coffee. It was ok with me though because it allowed me to catch up on all of my household duties. They are constantly put on hold over several days and sometimes weeks, when my level of fatigue is so severe that I become incapacitated and reside in my bed.

May – I started taking a drug called Anafranil to combat the OCD symptoms which had escalated to an all time high. After three weeks of slowly ramping up the dose, the side effects were so severe that the negative out-weighed the positive. I experienced tremendous hot flashes, trembling hands and weight-gain. I also cut my fingernails to the skin, to deter me from scratching. In addition, my doctor and I slowly started to decrease the dose of Adderall, as we thought it was probably responsible for the increase of the OCD symptoms. Finally, I was weaned off of Lexapro and transitioned into a new experiment with the drugs; Luvox, Zyprexa, Strattera, Anafranil, and Geodon.

I felt like such a lab rat at times, but I remained determined to be proactive as opposed to being reactive. It was at this time that I jumped in with both feet and researched all I could about my illnesses. I purchased several self-help books; Bipolar Disorder Survival Guide, The OCD Workbook and You Mean I'm Not Crazy, Lazy or Stupid? As I delved into reading these books, my monthly journaling stopped.

In 2005 I was taking five different medications a day. We went back to Zoloft for depression to see if my body would respond better, Depakote to control my manic episodes, Concerta for the ADD symptoms, Risperdal for OCD and Clonazepam to use as a muscle relaxant and sleep aid. In September of that year I weighed 156 lbs. The ADD symptoms I was battling at that time were; severe short-term memory loss, extreme fatigue, I was slow to process basic information, lacked motivation and was often forgetful. I also had very low self-esteem and exhibited signs of impulsiveness. The symptoms of OCD I had to cope with were brutal bouts of obsessive skin picking, increased appetite and severe weight gain, constant hand washing and I was overly concerned with order, symmetry and exactness. The side effects I was experiencing at this point were heavy and achy legs, which prevented me from being able to get out of bed in the morning.

One year later I learned that I had acquired yet another label - Restless Leg Syndrome (RLS). RLS is a neurological condition that is characterized by the irresistible urge to move the legs. Creepy-crawly and gnawing sensations prevented me from being able to fall asleep at night. I would often find myself bike riding or shopping at the 24 hour Wal-Mart at two or three in the morning. It is a horrible condition!

I also had periods of deep apathy, where I didn't care about anything. Severe daily fatigue attacks and short-term memory loss played a large part in losing my fulltime job in sales. To function even at a minimum, I had to take two to three naps a day.

Staying on and completing a task was still difficult, as I was easily distracted by other things I had to attend to. I attempted to organize and prioritize, but I would eventually get overwhelmed with what was at hand. I would then get frustrated and feel sorry for myself; I would go to sleep to "Escape!" This has been my greatest struggle.

In 2006 the regimen of my daily medications were as follows…

Concerta – 36mg ER Tablets – (2 x's daily)
- (Morning dose @ 6:00A.M.), (Afternoon dose @ 2:00P.M.)
- A mild central nervous system stimulant used to treat ADD.
- *Side-Effects: Trembling hands and racing heart*

Zoloft – 300mg Tabs (once daily)
- (Evening dose @ Bedtime)
- Selective Serotonin Reuptake Inhibitor (SSRI) used to treat depression and to act as a mood enhancer

Depakote – 500mg Tablets (2 x's daily)
- (Afternoon dose @ 5:00P.M.), (Evening dose @ Bedtime)
- Anti-convulsant & anti-manic used to treat Mania.
- *Side-Effects: Headaches, Missed Periods*

I still suffered from the repulsive skin picking. My legs were disgusting and I had a very poor self-image. "Who lives in Florida and can't wear shorts or a bathing suit?" "I CAN'T!"

My excessive concern with order, symmetry and exactness continued. I would check and re-check the things I did all day long, yet I still found it difficult to keep my home in order.

The symptoms of social anxiety disorder increased about this time as well. I found it very hard to even answer a ringing phone so it often went unanswered. Family members and friends became concerned. I also avoided going to the mailbox, for fear that a neighbor might want to engage in conversation. I couldn't even plan a lunch date because of the energy it would require. We stopped going to church because once again, I wasn't able to handle the incredible amount of mental and physical energy it took to simply get ready. Also, after the services I found myself walking swiftly to the car to avoid fellowshipping with the parishioners.

Early in 2007 my cocktail was once again re-evaluated:
- Zoloft – 100mg twice a day - (For Depression)
- Depakote – 1,000mg once a day - (For Mania)
- Concerta – 36mg twice a day – (For ADD)
- Risperdal – 1mg twice a day – (For OCD & Anxiety)
- Clonazepam – 0.5mg – (Tranquilizer For Sleeplessness)

Several months later we once again shuffled the deck, and this time I introduced an herbal remedy called Valerian, to combat my sleeplessness. It worked very well and was comforting to find a safe alternative for the tranquilizer.

As I write the last words in this chapter, I am thrilled to tell you that I am doing amazingly well. I can't remember when my last bout of depression was. I can also tell you that my mania has stabilized and I feel very "in control" of my thoughts, words and actions. The focus and attention on typing this page is clear and sharp. To my dismay though, I will be brutally honest with you. The elation I have for feeling so well - increases the flow of adrenaline - thus, I just spent the past ten minutes ripping open soars on my legs. The fight goes on.

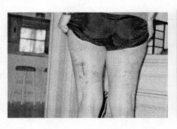 

I was bored, so I started picking.   Time consuming bandaging.

CHAPTER SEVEN

Social Anxiety Disorder

I have come to understand that anxiety is a complicated byproduct of bipolar disorder. Throughout my life I have experienced immense anxiety, but it has been more prominent in my adult years. As I look back, my anxiety attacks seem to have something to do with an overwhelming feeling of guilt and/or embarrassment. I can't explain what might have been the trigger(s), but deep sadness, impulsivity and immediate action, was the recipe for the following stories.

In the early nineties, my boyfriend Matthew took me with him on a business trip to Hawaii of all places. We were having a wonderful time and really enjoying ourselves, when out of the blue I began to feel guilty that he was paying my way. I was immediately consumed with despair and wanted to get back home to my comfort zone. I wasn't able to shake off the gloom for the remainder of the week, but we toughed it out.

The following year, my first boyfriend in Atlanta invited me to come on vacation with him to Panama City, Florida. We rented a condo on the beach for an extended weekend. Unfortunately, the first night we were there, it happened again. This time the discomfort was unbearable and my tears would not stop flowing. I convinced Rich that I couldn't fight it and that we needed to drive the three hours back home <u>that</u> night! He was furious and this episode started the demise of our relationship.

Another similar incident occurred when I was dating my future husband, David. I was leery about going to Jamaica with him and told him the story of my past travel mishaps. He assured me that everything would be fine and that he'd take care of me should I begin to feel unwell. Then, it happened again! Suddenly, for no reason at all, I spiraled down and became depressed. How could I be so blessed to have these traveling opportunities, but not have the capacity to enjoy them? I still don't understand what happened to me in those instances, so I've learned to just leave it to God because I know He has all the answers.

Here's another example: just after our second child, Sierra, was born, David and I hired a painter for the interior of our home. The man was easy to work with and was doing a fantastic job, but near the end, I began to feel uncomfortable around him. He smiled a lot and always wanted to talk to me. David thought that the painter had developed a crush because I was always so accommodating.

The day <u>after</u> the job was finished; the painter rang our door bell and was holding a single red rose. I watched him from a window, but did not open the door. I was scared to death! A whirlwind of negative thoughts entered my mind and I immediately called the police. By the time David got home from work, my anxiety level was through the roof. I forced him to come with me and the children and spend the night at a girlfriend's house. He was sure that I was making something out of nothing. Of course he thought that I was being silly, but he came anyway so that I would calm down and relax. The police did talk with the painter and nothing ever came of it.

The next episode lasted only a short while, not more than several hours, instead of several days. In a sudden attack, I could actually feel a chemical change and a surge of high energy consume me. It took only a few moments to turn my life upside down. Unexpectedly, I decided to throw my marriage into a state of separation, move myself and the kids to Nashville, Tennessee and work for a temp agency. I would also pursue my singing career. As David walked in the door from a long day at the office, I unloaded on him.

We didn't know it at the time, but in retrospect we recognize this incident as a text book manic episode. David patiently listened to me rant and rave about my newly devised plan, and watched as I went on and on. His cool, calm and collected response to the situation was the big key to getting things back in order. That evening I started packing.

At bed time, I was once again struck with an intense chemical mood change. I began to cry uncontrollably and struggled for every breath. My mind and my heart were battling it out. Thankfully, my mission collapsed and dissolved because during the emotional turmoil, I came to my senses. As I gasped for air, I woke David and told him that I had been experiencing a severe anxiety attack, and that I had no intention of leaving and starting a new life. I didn't know what had come over me.

One very important lesson we learned from that experience was the way that David responded to my irrational behavior. Instead of "freaking out" or becoming domineering, he calmly went along with wherever I verbally took him. If he had reacted in a defensive mode, I would have developed a steely reserve and it would have taken much longer for me to "come to."

In 2005, we got new next door neighbors. Conversations and time would reveal that they were not the most ideal next door family. I conducted an internet search on the mother and father and found that they both had police records that were several pages long. Offenses ranged from drug possession and distribution to grand theft. For the next year, I became a home body and was ultra sensitive regarding our safety. I convinced David to upgrade the security lighting around all four sides of the house. I also found myself putting up curtains and peeking out of my windows to track the comings and goings of their visitors. When it was apparent that exchanges were being made in their driveway, we got the police involved. That family eventually moved out and I gratefully gave up the life of a recluse.

CHAPTER EIGHT

Attention Deficit Disorder (ADD)

The symptoms of Attention Deficit Disorder (ADD), were noticeable in my elementary school years, but I wasn't properly diagnosed until many years later. I was simply labeled LD, a student that demonstrated learning disabilities. This label was incredibly tough on my self-esteem. Inattention, hyperactivity and impulsive behavior were the major symptoms. To this day I often have trouble finishing tasks because my mind wanders and I am not able to maintain focus. Quite often I notice that I am tapping my fingers or feet or bouncing my legs. The writing of this book has been twenty years in the making for these very reasons.

Impulsivity is something I struggle with quite a bit. I recall one day in particular when I took unnecessary risk. I was driving out of a shopping center parking lot and slammed the gas pedal to the floor. I drove recklessly into traffic, and then pulled into another parking lot to catch my breath and analyze what I had just done. It was like I was "outside of myself." I know that God's angels were with me because thankfully, that episode lasted less than five minutes.

Very often I have mood swings, a quick temper, low tolerance for stress and as I've already demonstrated, problems with relationships. I firmly believe that ADD is partly to blame for these issues. My marriage is nothing short of a roller coaster ride, as my emotions daily wreak havoc on the two of us.

On September 12, 2005, I struggled to get through a typical day of being "un-medicated" and suffered tremendously. Trying to function was an absolute nightmare. My bipolar symptoms seemed to be well balanced and under control with Zoloft and Depakote, but the symptoms of my other mood disorders increased in their intensity.

I decided to spend the day focused on completing backed up paper work and armed myself with a priority list, colored labels and highlighters. These tools are absolutely essential in assisting me with the most simplistic routine.

As I headed for my desk, I noticed that the kitchen counter was still a mess from the night before. I decided to do a quick cleanup and in the process, noticed that my plants needed watering. I filled the watering can, and then reminded myself to get back on track with my original task of tackling backed up paperwork. The phone rang and of course, I got caught up in a conversation. Finally I made it to my desk and started sorting and labeling folders. I became perplexed as to how or where to file a particular document. My hand found its way to my chin while I was thinking. I felt a bumpy spot and got an overwhelming urge to scrape it off with my fingernail. This urge consumed me so much, that I got up and went to the bathroom mirror. It is here that I spent a considerable amount of time inspecting and picking at my face.

Not being strong enough to control that behavior, I was left feeling guilty and ashamed. I then became sad and discouraged. My body and mind were consumed with severe fatigue. This exhaustion caused me to go to bed, as sleep has **ALWAYS** been my emotional escape.

A couple of hours later, I woke up and once again had feelings of guilt; about the time I wasted by sleeping. I got determined and decided to make up for lost time and do something productive to validate my day. I also knew that I needed to do something physically active, so I could have solid rest come nightfall. I noticed that the grass had gotten tall, so I headed out to mow the lawn. Meanwhile, my backed up paperwork was still sitting in piles on and around my desk.

Once I got back indoors, I felt wiped out again. To avoid another nap, I went to find some caffeine. I got back on track and headed toward my desk. On the way though, I noticed that the carpet needed cleaning, so I went to the utility room and grabbed the spot remover and vacuum. I only had enough energy to do that one area.

Then I needed to take a seat and rest, so I decided to check my e-mail at the same time. Of course I found something there that I needed to respond to, so I spent even more time away from my original task of organizing my backed up paperwork.

Two o'clock rolled around and in my mind, I had wasted the entire morning. The kids jumped off the school bus and the rest of the day was dedicated to helping them complete their homework assignments, chores and outside activities.

When my husband got home that evening, I was wiped out and in bed, picking the sores on my legs. I wasn't able to prepare a proper dinner, so I was once again overwhelmed with feelings of guilt and told myself that I was not a good wife! David on the other hand, stepped up to the plate as he always has, and prepared a nourishing meal for the family.

In 2006 I went looking for a part-time job. The simple task of filling out applications was daunting, as my thought processing was not swift or sharp. I was terribly embarrassed and requested to take the applications home to complete. Limited memory retention of simple directions, short-term memory loss and the inability to recall dates, names and specific work experiences discouraged me greatly. I gave up looking for part-time work and shifted my attention toward completing this book.

CHAPTER NINE

Obsessive Compulsive Disorder (OCD) / Self Injury

During my early thirties, I developed another disorder called Obsessive Compulsive Disorder or OCD. My gut and intuition tell me that this exhaustive suffering is a side effect of one or more of my medications. My doctors don't have a clue.

I have learned from the Mayo Clinic website that obsessions are recurrent, persistent, unwanted ideas, thoughts or impulses that I experience involuntarily. They commonly intrude when I am trying to concentrate on other things. Fear of dirt or contamination, concern with order, symmetry and exactness and fear of harming myself - are the obsessions I personally struggle with.

The compulsions are repetitive behaviors that I am driven to perform regularly to combat the obsessions. These include; excessive hand washing, arranging items in a precise order, and touching certain objects several times. This sickness is deeply rooted in anxiety. When I perform these rituals, I usually feel some relief from anxiety, but not for long. The discomfort returns and I am compelled to repeat the awful behavior over and over again. My biggest complaint with this illness is that the rituals take up more and more of my day, making it virtually impossible to lead a "normal" life.

In my thirties and early forties, obsessive skin picking has controlled my life. My suspicion is that the compulsion to pick is a side effect of my ADD medication, as it has a tendency to increase my adrenalin level. I have also noticed that my hands tremble. My legs look disgusting and I have a very poor self image.

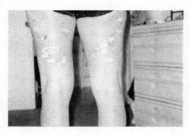

Bandaged Wounds

Bloody Band-Aids

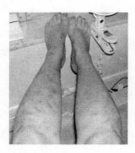

Raw Shins

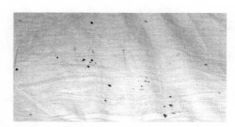

Blood Stained Bed Sheets

These behaviors interfere with everyday functioning. Checking and re-checking things I do all day long is a hassle and very time consuming. I possess an excessive concern with order, symmetry and exactness; yet I still can't keep up with simple household chores. My husband and children are a tremendous help in this area, but I do carry a heavy load of guilt that I am not able to be more self sufficient.

CHAPTER TEN

Letting Go and Letting God

In 2004, I told my husband that I wanted a trial separation. David was out of the country working in Guam. I wasn't brave enough to tell him over the phone and so I ended up faxing the shocking news to him. In the letter I explained that I had "lost" myself and couldn't find any happiness in our loveless marriage.

You would think that I would be depressed at this big move, but in actuality, I was manic and quite pumped up! I felt a much needed sense of control over my life and surrendered our marriage to God. I submerged myself in contemporary Christian music and never felt closer to my Lord than I did then. It gave me great strength, understanding and resolve.

I rented an apartment close to our home. Our children were four and five at this time and came away from the experience unscathed. I never said an unkind word to them about their father, as he was and still is a wonderful father. I worked very hard to make the whole moving experience nothing more than a great adventure for them. I thank God that that's how they both remember it.

After three months there were many issues that still needed to be tackled before I was willing to give the marriage another try. I have chosen not to go into detail on the negative issues, as that information has no place in this writing. I will confess though that my irritability level was so high, that I actually asked my therapist if it was possible to be allergic to a human being.

David is a wonderful provider and is completely committed and devoted to us as a family unit. The children adore him and I love their relationship. He is knowledgeable and diligent with our finances and is also handy around the house, yard and with the family vehicles.

Last and certainly not least, David is truly a gentle man. During our courtship, he encouraged me when I had depressive episodes and he was also able to calm me through the manic ones. I had my share of boyfriends prior to meeting my husband, but I know without a doubt that God planned our union.

Blessed Union

CHAPTER ELEVEN

Nothing Short of a Miracle

Prayer works! After three months of separation, God had performed a miracle! I found myself falling in love with a new person, a man of God who wanted to "give" of his time, skill and money to others in need. I found myself physically, emotionally and mentally attracted to my changed husband. As David grew closer to the Lord, he allowed Him to work through him. I am convinced more than ever that the decision to separate was God's plan. I consider it nothing short of a miracle, that we were able to pull things together. We didn't view our new growth as rekindling a romance, but as a brand new love and appreciation for each other.

I now carefully track my "emotional cycle" and its symptoms. I know that the true "Yo" loves David and wants very much to make the marriage work. I have learned that "love" is a decision and not a feeling. So, I have decided to love, to be thoughtful, to be affectionate, to be considerate and to respect my husband.

I am very proud of and happy to be with David and I am honored to be his wife. I have also learned that separation and divorce can be contagious. There were so many broken relationships around me at that time, that that environment weakened my own personal belief system.

Still, even with this very valuable lesson learned, I have no regrets for taking the drastic action I took. I now have a happy and peaceful heart. David's efforts and commitment have been remarkable. I enjoy his company, and his "3-part dates" should be shared with the entire dating world! We're enjoying conversing, pampering and snuggling. We now share in common the children, the same music, goals for our future, The "Yo" Show, a renewed passion for dancing together (how we met), and a newly committed church life.

We're getting closer to knowing each others' hearts and souls. We agreed to let God guide us in the move to Florida. It was imperative to do this, so that it would help us not to fall into the old patterns of our negative life in Georgia. Amazingly we even re-established regular domestic duties. We agreed that if I started to feel overwhelmed, I could hire the help I needed, but would search for that help first with church members and include David in the pricing process. This arrangement was a giant step for us. David now understands and is sensitive to why house work may not get done in "his" timeframe, but knows I will complete all of my chores in "my" timeframe.

We took an Intimate Marriage Course and learned how to introduce romance into the relationship. In a two week period, we did almost fifteen "date like" things. Prior to the separation, that would have taken about 3 years to accomplish! We went to restaurants and focused on enjoying each others' company, not how much the bill was going to be. I would still like to rent a movie or go to a theater sometime together. David just doesn't like to sit still for long periods of time, so I guess I'll have to let this wish go.

I am making "baby steps" to learn how to care for my husband, when he will allow it. I have started by respecting and listening to him, putting his clean clothes away and being able to show him affection. If he gets sick, I know that I will be a loving nurse.

His intense focus on money has relaxed. I have agreed to use coupons and go to the warehouse stores whenever possible. We also compiled a new household budget together. By being "right" with God, the issue of being a man of integrity has taken care of itself. He agreed to let me donate DJ services when I feel that it is appropriate - and I agreed to take only the "high end" paying gigs - so that I can be home more often.

I am being a wonderful wife and love my new roles in our marriage. We have become each other's best friend again. For instance, I was able to respond lovingly to a beautiful greeting card he had left on my steering wheel, when before I would have faked a "thank you" and just dismissed it.

I've always known that David's love for me was complete and unending, but now I see it, feel it and accept it. I proudly brag on him to friends and neighbors when he has a commitment at the church. It warms my heart and makes my love for him increase, each time he goes. He has transformed from a man who takes and keeps for himself, to a man of compassion and who gives to others. This was the big key to my returning home.

CHAPTER TWELVE

Stabilization in a Psychiatric Hospital

Late in 2002 I suffered the absolute worst bout of depression you can possibly imagine. For the first time as a result of my mental illness, I was hospitalized. I admitted myself for five days, which was the minimum time the facility allowed. Easter of 2003 came and I relapsed. This time I spent ten days in the infirmary. Both times were triggered by extreme stress as I was not able to function normally from day to day.

This overwhelming stress was brought on by several things, and as I look back on that time, I see that I was experiencing life changing events. David and I had reunited from a trial separation and agreed to give our marriage a second chance. In addition to that, he accepted a job transfer to another state. So not only was our marriage on delicate ground, but we jumped into a whirlwind of preparing our Georgia home for sale and looking for a new home in Florida. With that came packing for the move, the move itself and unpacking in the new home. Adding insult to injury, this was all done in a timeframe of two weeks. This toxic combination was a roller coaster ride that took its toll on me both mentally and physically. I simply collapsed and was completely out of commission.

David drove me to the hospital and once I got there, I waited for what seemed like forever to be interviewed by a case worker. It was his job to evaluate the severity of my mental and emotional state. More importantly from the hospitals viewpoint, to make sure that I had insurance that would pay for my stay. I was shocked to learn that if I didn't have health insurance, the hospital would not accept me. Upon admittance, I was escorted to the adult unit. It was adjacent to the high risk unit and both doors posted signs that read – "Split Risk." I was frightened!

The front desk staff stripped me of all freedom. They took away my purse and its contents, my jewelry, makeup, day planner and cell phone. The days ahead held wakeup calls at 6:00A.M. for needle pricks. Blood tests were ongoing for drugs. Three times a day we were able to walk as a group to the cafeteria, only to find institutional food awaiting our hunger pangs. It was as close to being in prison as I ever want to be. No words I might write could truly describe it.

There was a myriad of characters in the adult unit. I remember them vividly. Diane was in her early 40's and she was unstable every day that I was there; constantly crying and loudly verbalizing "I want to go home!" She actually tried to escape! She is what the facility called, a "runner." One day we were heading for lunch when she darted out of our single file line. She made a mad dash across the field, reached the exterior fence, took her shoes off and managed to climb a quarter of the way up until one of the guards caught her. Her actions riled up everyone in my group, some even cheered her on. Personally, I was scared.

Sue was in her early 50's and was my roommate for the first night I was there. Thankfully the next day she was transferred to the "High Risk Unit," as she proved to be too difficult to control. The next two nights I actually had some privacy, with the room to myself.

Patty, my second roommate, was very nice. She appeared to be in her 40's. Her nose was in a book for the entire week. The book's subject was how to start a home based business and before she left the hospital, she had decided to become a special events planner. We talked about networking together for my DJ business, but we never actually exchanged contact information.

Beth was in her mid 30's. The patients all judged and stereotyped this woman to be a "hooker," or at least she made herself look like one. Upon arrival, she wore a full length black fur coat and her face streamed of tears and ruined makeup.

There was a good looking young man named Ross. He was about 20 years of age and had no direction in his life. Prior to his stay at this facility, he had spent four years in prison. He ended up in the hospital after breaking his parole and urgently needed to learn how to manage his anger. He had no parents to guide him, only an aunt who offered him a room. He dressed like a "trendy" teenager, wearing his pants half way down his backside. He was constantly pulling them up. During "group," he usually displayed a bad attitude and didn't want to participate in the discussion or activity.

Cheryl was in her early 40's and she impressed me quite a bit. She was one of the top salespeople for a nutrition company. We talked a lot and she even tried to recruit me. Cheryl was there for depression and with good reason. Her husband had told her that he was leaving her and the kids. In spite of the depression I could see that her personality was positive and upbeat.

Robert looked as though he was in his late sixties, but I'm sure he was much younger. He exhibited the odd signs of Alzheimer's. After three days in the Adult Unit he was transferred to the High Risk Unit and put on suicide watch. Robert was very talkative and he drove us nuts, (please pardon the pun). Just the same, we were all saddened to see how this man had to live without normal brain functioning.

There was one man who barely said a word to anyone. He appeared to be in his mid 40's. Vance just stared at the floor and only spoke when the staff required him to.

Lori was in her early 30's. This poor woman latched on to me and anyone else who would give her the time of day. She suffered from severe depression and an incredible amount of other health problems. Her self-esteem was very low, as she was 300 pounds of walking and talking negativism. I tried to be kind and lend an ear when I thought I could handle it. Honestly though, I found myself trying to hide from her or pretend to be asleep, when she would come knocking.

Several times a day we were required to do simplistic, childlike activities such as coloring or cutting and pasting magazine pictures. We were instructed to do these exercises to express and deal with how we were feeling. The fruit of our labor was analyzed and discussed with us by the psychiatrist.

One of my greatest struggles at the hospital was attempting to regulate my body clock. Depression kept me in bed for many hours at a time. I would find myself trying to sleep during the day (even though the staff discouraged it.) At night I would lie awake tired and frustrated, as the nurse would not allow me to have something that would help me sleep. I was miserable.

Smoking breaks were scheduled throughout the day for the patients who required it, and this was the majority. Even though I didn't smoke, I sometimes joined them because it meant ten minutes of outside time in the air and sunshine. "Group" was held several times a day to verbally share and express how and what we were feeling and how best to deal with difficult emotions.

When I first entered this psychiatric facility, my outlook on life was absolutely hopeless. I constantly thank God that I emerged from the experience, stable, strong, and with great hope for my future. He continues to bless me, my family and those with whom I share my story.

CHAPTER THIRTEEN

Hurricane Season 2004

Hurricane Frances Approaches Florida
(Credit: NASA, NOAA)

The storm season of 2004 pummeled South Florida with massive destruction. Hurricanes Charley, Frances, Ivan and Jeanne attacked our home and safety, as well as our mental and physical wellbeing. These four record breaking storms came and went from mid-August to late September. That six week period was one of the most difficult times of my life. Even pregnancy and delivery didn't come close to the trauma I experienced then.

At this time I was forced to learn many things about myself and my illness. The most important lesson, was to always have enough medication on hand for emergency purposes.

As the news reports became increasingly grim, my husband and I worked feverishly to prepare the children to leave and to board up the house. Residents were encouraged to either leave the area or go to a Red Cross shelter. We chose to make the three hour drive across the state to Naples, where we could stay at David's fathers' winter home.

I was a little panicky, but kept it together as best as I could. My main motivation was to not worry the kids. Also, I was preparing to travel alone for a gig in Virginia. It was my own 20 year high school reunion and I had volunteered my D.J. services. I began to suffer severe anxiety attacks as I became increasingly aware that I was not going to be able to make the trip. The guilt I felt for letting the organizers down was tremendous. They had trusted and relied on me to make the event musically memorable - and I dropped the ball! The best thing I could do was to overnight, all of my cd's from the early 1980's. In the end everything worked out for them, but I was a wreck.

I became increasingly depressed, and began to run out of my medications. This situation got even worse and I became bedridden for several weeks. It was very difficult to do, but we were eventually able to buy some antidepressants at an urgent care clinic in Naples. The doctor who examined me also prescribed a tranquilizer to help me sleep through the night.

It was a blessing that our family cat Co-Co was with us. She was very pregnant and about to deliver her litter at any moment. When she did, it was an all day affair. Since I was bed bound, my children delivered the four kittens. I was able to rest and the kids were occupied with the wonder of birth. They continue to treasure and carry the memory of that experience even today.

When we returned home, I called my doctor and several others to once again get regulated on a medication regimen. So much storm damage had been done that no one was yet open for business. The Red Cross had even set up shop on my street to feed my family and our neighbors. They also supplied crisis counselors for those needing the service. It took a long three weeks, but I was finally able to get an appointment with a walk-in clinic just one town away. They were kind, patient and understanding.

The greatest advice I can pass on to others with mental illness, is the importance of finding a psychiatrist that you feel comfortable with. Additionally, it is vital that together you experiment with and closely monitor different medications. Once you find the right cocktail for your chemical makeup, stick to it at all costs and don't find yourself in the dangerous situation of running out. Finally, just because you're feeling good, does not mean that you should stop taking your medication(s). **<u>YOU'RE FEELING GOOD "BECAUSE" YOUR MED.'S ARE WORKING!</u>**

CHAPTER FOURTEEN

The Stigma and Helping Others

Rosalynn Carter, (President Carter's wife), has dedicated the past thirty years of her life to help break the stigma of mental illness. In an interview she gave to CNN, she said, "The stigma is still so pervasive, it keeps people from going for help." "They don't want to be labeled mentally ill." "We have to overcome that."

She and her staff at the Carter Center in Georgia, work diligently to educate the public. They encourage people to learn the real facts - that mental illnesses are biological like any other illnesses - and there should be no distinction between physical illness, mental illness and other illnesses. I sent Mrs. Carter an early working copy of this book and she sent a thank-you note back saying that she was glad to have it.

Famous individuals such as; Terry Bradshaw (football player), Jimi Hendrix, and Winston Churchill have battled bipolar disorder throughout their lives. Patty Duke (actress), took the bull by the horns and wrote a book called **A Brilliant Madness**...*Living With Manic-Depressive Illness.* She has been a huge inspiration to me in writing my own memoirs on the subject.

Writing this book has provided me wonderful therapy, in and of itself. I enjoy offering help and hope to others by telling my story, mostly to teens. I am also pursuing the lecture and talk show circuits. Early in 2008, I sent this book to: The Montel Williams Show, The Tyra Banks Show, The Dr. Phil Show, Fox & Friends, The View, Good Morning America, Larry King Live and of course…to Oprah!

Below is a letter from the grandmother I met only once in my life. Together in France, she and her two young sons, (one being my Papa) survived the holocaust.

May 28, 1992

Dear Yo!
    I like "Yolande" very much but you like Yo, so it is! I do not want to interfere.
    Thank you very much for your fine letter and the beautiful picture of you. I like it very much and can judge you beautiful.
    Like you I think Oprah would be the person to see. I like the way she does her show. She is an intelligent person. Just keep her interested in you. You have a lot to offer.
    Today is our 44th year anniversary. It does not seem so much to us as we get along fine.
    Vermont is where my husband was born. It is a pleasant place and I do not care for the changes of temperature with my delicate heart. But it is beautiful at all seasons. I particularly have admired the fall.
    Everyday Wayne takes me walking as it is my doctor's order. I passed a lot of time at the hospital for that heart of mine. I am 89 years old since the 2nd of May. Just think how old I am. Well I have had a very interesting life also but now I am quietly settled with a lot of souvenirs. Now I have to take care of my heart.
    My husband Wayne is a wonderful man but we are poor and that is not fun. Because of it I appreciate my husband who does all he can to make me well and happy.
    I cannot write too long and have to say that I love to read about you and since I look at Oprah I hope to see you with her soon.

I love you very much. - Louise

CHAPTER FIFTEEN

The "Yo" Show

National Anthem Performances

Atlanta Fulton County Stadium –   *DJ "Yo" -*

The Omni –   *The Georgia Dome –*

Yolande "Yo" Fawcett is the consummate entertainment professional. Whether singing the National Anthem to capacity crowds of 50,000 or simply entertaining an intimate gathering of family, friends and guests, she always delivers a spectacular performance. With over 13 years of professional entertainment experience and equipped with only the very best in high end audio, "Yo" has all of the tools necessary to insure that each of her clients events are a huge success.

As Florida's Singing DJ and Party Motivator, "Yo" is one of the Treasure Coast's most in demand entertainers. Ideal for corporate events, wedding ceremonies and receptions, private parties, class and family reunions, birthdays, Bar/Bat Mitzvah's, religious ceremonies, holiday festivities and numerous other functions, The "Yo" Show is a one of a kind entertainment experience.

Offering a variety of services and packages, The "Yo" Show features one of Florida's largest collections of popular music available. Armed with this library of hit songs from the 40's to today's current hits - add an equally eclectic selection of karaoke music - and you've got the makings of a spectacular dance floor!

"Yo" has the knowledge, the professional DJ skills, the vocal talent and the right sound equipment to complement and create the perfect mood for any occasion. From the very formal and elegant, to the casual and upbeat party atmosphere, "Yo" will insure that your party or special event is one to treasure.

When "Yo" discovered that her God-given talent to entertain could lift spirits and help others in need, she made a conscience decision to donate her services whenever possible. The following is a short list of these performances: The September 11th Relief Fund, Big Brothers and Big Sisters, The National Breast

Cancer Coalition, The Hosea Williams Feed the Hungry & Homeless Foundation, The Atlanta Community Food Bank, The Boys and Girls Clubs of America, Easter Seals and The National Alzheimer's Association.

In 1999 "Yo" was inspired to orchestrate a fund raising event that she titled _THE "YO" SHOW FOR KOSOVO_. Many families were displaced from the Balkans and eventually found themselves in Atlanta, Georgia of all places. The money and humanitarian items collected went to benefit the war torn refugees.

Organized a 24-Hour Karaoke event to support the Kosovar Refugees.

- <u>NOTES</u> -